BLUE MONDAY

The Wesleyan Poetry Program: Volume 70

Blue Monday

by CALVIN FORBES

*For Gary Gildner
+ muse power —

11/24/76

Calvin Forbes*

WESLEYAN UNIVERSITY PRESS

Middletown, Connecticut

Acknowledgement is gratefully made to the New American Library and to Random House, the publishers of anthologies in which several of the poems in this book first appeared; and to the following periodicals, in the pages of which other poems first appeared: *The American Scholar, The Emerson Review, Monmouth Review, Omega, Plowshares, Poetry, Survival, Words* and *The Yale Review.*

The poems 'The Chocolate Soldiers', 'Gabriel's Blues', 'Good Morning Blues' and 'Poem on My Birthday' were first published in *Poetry.*

Library of Congress Cataloging in Publication Data

Forbes, Calvin, 1945–
Blue Monday.

(The Wesleyan poetry program, v. 70)
Poems.
I.   Title.
PS3556.066B5   811'.5'4   73–15011
ISBN 0–8195–2070–5
ISBN 0–8195–1070–x   (pbk.)

Manufactured in the United States of America
First edition

FOR MY MOTHER, FATHER

JANE AND TARA

Contents

I

For You

Going to bed I bump into the dark,
I stumble to the west and to the east.
Sugar the train is gone
And I fall on the beach of sister night.

Come away from the streets where you
Claw your childhood out of the
Sidewalk and come see
About me, about the way I used to be . . .

Last night I knew I wasn't about to be
Delivered so I went to church
And I went to court and so
Once more I rode you past the final stop.

You better go back to the ghetto, back
To where you belong; no more honey
In your tea; you better
Take two lumps of sugar and be glad you're

My only one: and so be kind to me before
It rises again, before I'm dripping
And running wild through
The layers of secrets trying to drown you.

Going to bed I bump into the dark.
My feelings are memories I lean on; they're
Lines I follow back to you.
You pull me up towards your soft shadow.

Home

Blue sky blue water
And the keys to home jingle nearby.

You won't see my tracks
But in the mud I hunt the ocean.

A breath ago I was plowing
And then like a deacon I heard again

The gift of a thousand
Tongues. Nose to wind I glided

To Big Apple shaking
Dirt and full of feathers; I left

Worries south for another
Mule. Daily I'm due like a rooster

But before I return
You watch this eagle drink the sky.

On one wing I could fly
To the lost shore where beauty lives

Within my memory
Where the Captain first stole my voice.

Some children belong
In the yard, others wander in the wilds.

But whose father
Will lift me and help me run this race?

Negro Knees

Negro knees I have seen are pears:
Thigh to calf sloping together.
Slowly slender dark limbs

Without knots or wrinkles. Bending
Over the water, she has branches
On both shores.

Fashion says she walks perfect knees:
Bones with bridges and no gulf for
The skin to ford. As she

Walks in the bus station the drivers
Raise their voices and her Negro
Knees bend as she disappears

Into her sleep lifting the centuries.
One knee under the other Negro
Knee which is half a pear.

Potlicker Blues

Momma a carrot grows underground
Alone very blind like an island seeing
No other but itself; and it always looks old
Wrinkled, as if its youth had been bitter.

But shame a country girl like you
Thought they grew on trees like oranges.
And you peel carrots like their skin
Were evil: didn't your Momma teach you nothing?

The old people wanted to boil the bad
Taste away; or at least they thought every-
Thing green and fresh was raw—
To be treated in the same manner as pork.

And maybe overcooked collards explains why
Granny looked so dried out by the time
She was ready for the grave;
Even if she drank only potlicker, and never good

Cornlicker, getting juiced off the vitamins.
Tender vegetables won't hurt your gums.
And Momma they got frozen greens now;
And you know you can't buy potlicker at the A&P.

The Hours

In the morning cool and slender, you
Haunt the hours I'm blind in; you shoot
The night. I'm on a diet of beer; I'm
Cold; the weather tutors me with the dry
Smell of cow dung that lights me when
I fantasize I'm foreign. Your grey eyes

Dull the crayon sun. How crazy I am today!
This pasture isn't home but the months
Go on like an elephant's skin. The weight
Of my sleep makes me stumble as I soothe
My exploding bones; the hot sting of beer
Rises like a fire torn from me again where
I broke you in your belly. Daily you knock
Like a bandit, a ghost beating my heart.

Gabriel's Blues

Everyone's going to ride tomorrow
Though poor sons lie, steal; I know
The air of Jesus: whirling strongly,

Becoming a wall. Come to my comfort
Child and hear the horses in my head.
On the road read their direction; one

Ear lies unwounded: listen to the hoofs
From the other side of the world explode.
I know days when altars open like a mouth

Stretching our for air and sounds breaking
Become a shield bright below me while his
Dust and dirt blow into my trailing face.

The Chocolate Soldiers

Where's the winning without chocolate
I asked the General when the white bombs

Landed on Venus beach and the natives
Shot their tongues into our ears. Once

Chocolate was in front, and strangers
Bit what our hands extended, not laying

Us but we laying them in the dungy hay.
Brown candy melted in colonial mouths

When chocolate was sweet politics; white
Sons wrote home about Guam and bodies

With nude ankles. Now natives lay waste.
The brown will dominate even on Venus beach

Though I want to admit to taking my mirror
To insure courageous chocolate dwells there.

The Russian Poets

Coo wild bird coo
For you are a wild wish, finer
Outside the tenements than in God's forest.

The sound's gone where the Bird went
And I don't know what to say

But I saw you hug yourself now hug me.
My veins have nothing in them but blood
And I would stand in the empty

Space so that someone might be there once
It all came home again. I wish you
Could pull the shade; I wish to see you
When I sleep and life is low.

I think we're flying after something we
Already own, something very familiar.

But I'm on the Russian Poets instead of you
Because one of them said as he died:
'There are no more sounds worth hearing,
No mouth or ear worth while.'

I want to know what would bring a man
To sew his lip and clog himself
Until he's overflowing and flooded?

Can you feel the flight of the sounds?
Have you read the Russian Poets?

Get married to music, a drum inside,
Rhythm running down your thigh.
Bring something old and new, the country
And the town, the plow

And the switchblade, and let them be part
Of your city cry
Where all the Birds are shot down.

The Potter's Wheel

for Jane

I was mindless
As a lump of clay, drunk on gin
Until my kidneys ached,

The summer I met you.
I was the child, also master
With as many heads as a totem-pole;
But I denied you maternal

Pleasures by alternating my roles
Like a double agent.
Each time I'm almost forgotten I rise
Unexpectedly like a monadnock.

Soft in the center,
A blunt man whose life flattens
Near the edges,

I grow in your hands.
Everything changes except the shape
You give me.

The Other Side of This World

Put my glad rags in a cardboard box—
This old jiggerboo never grew mature.
Is everything in its place except me?
Don't be surprised; I called all day

And the only person I could reach was
The operator; and it's a sorry day when
Nothing is coming down but your foot.
And how deep is your stomach cause

That's how far your heart will fall!
When I'm gone I might come back cause
I'm always forgetting something special.
A crease in my overalls, my collar stiff,

I cried as many tears as I have teeth.
And I only got two in my mouth. Son of the
Sun look out: as you get black you burn.
Is everything in its place except me?

Dark Mirror

If I were from Timbuktu, perhaps
I should think the sea as mysterious
As the Sahara. Crossing water

In a hole of voices and fire eyes.
Inches apart but we can't see our bodies.
Only bright eyes and hearing

Continuous moans. My chains rattle
Like charms and we hide ourselves
In the darkness as if we were jackals.

I can't sleep. During the day we
Take a breath of air one by one up top.
You can see your shadow in the smooth ocean

If the big waves aren't bewitched.
But at night the air is dark
The ocean also and no one will see me.

II

Soledad

I smell water and I hear God knocking.
The way I feel tonight
The stars could be my mother's eyes
And go out and I wouldn't care.

People I eat music.
But sometimes I get weak
From laughing to myself and her face
Fades like a stranger's
And only the dusk reminds me of her lips.

I circle the night trying to ambush
The sky and closing my eyes No
Is the only word I hear.
It hurts to recall the origin of that echo.

As I retreat from the sound
And my soul leaks
My nose raw and open wide as Fifth Avenue
I wound easy
But in solitude I hum a bebop blues.

Listen someone's banging
And is it the rain?
She rode so smooth I soon forgot
My wild horse.
O Angela I rode my hearse into a lake!

My Marie

Let the rain darn my socks.
Outside on the clothes-line
They hang like sloths, upside
Down, a hole for a tongue.

Ah, a hole in the bottom
Means the water comes through
Like a river. Ah, a sock hole
Means there's a comparable
Hole in the worn and tired shoe.

When I walk now I can taste fallen
Ice-cream through my sole: I will know
Tears of ants when they're depressed.
As I stumble people will think
I'm spastic, or that I'm drunk,

A cripple anyway, impoverished!
Let the rain darn my socks.
I will catch a cold and die—
Or when I go and sweat in a gym
They will get soggy and embarrass me.

Ah, failure of belief. My poor socks
Have outgrown their feet! They will
Have to be taken off like the skin
Of a bear that's needed for a rug.

Let the rain darn my socks.
Let me be an altar as you slip
The wafer into someone's sore mouth.
I'll only watch; I'm old lollipop ears.
I will hide in a beard of rain awaiting

Your sweet kiss. When you finally hear
My cough, dice will be dropped by God.
We'll be as lucky as the Jews. We'll know
How to grow wise together in a desert.

Wedding Song

Leda, if you'll be my wife
Let's end the swan's flight
And put his feathers in your
Hair. Though always a lord

I wouldn't be a good priest
And mornings I find I'm weak
From the angel who's my beast.
For you I give up knowledge.

Now that no child weighs on your
Breast, let me forsake my power.
If a body upon a body is one glory
Then Leda let us go and be merry.

Dreaming of Mao

On the river a canoe of coconuts
Sails for China. Men want to
See Mao and wear pajamas

And slant their eyes so they'll be wise.
Though the navigator crosses his
Stars, they land in Jersey

City and their blond comrades feed them
Fried chicken; they wanted waving
Chinese children, millions

Singing in unison and not a waitress
Yelling toast a BLT. But the ship
Is being eaten by a monkey.

Walking home thinking Taoism, Maoism, so
Confused they wonder if ideology
Is a form of fantasy.

My Father's House

1908–1970

I live quietly and go nowhere
And this house shakes like a tree.
Open the door, Jesus is the hinge
Squeaking from the rusty rain.

Deadheart, this house wasn't built
By human hands, and no bricks will
You find, wood or glass. This house
Stands like a skeleton inside the worst

Possible skin. Knock and enter afraid,
Your shadow rigid as the brass laid
Across your coffin. Come closer and see
Broken beams, a sacred slum, no mystery

Except memory. Rise and make ends meet
My tenant. Safe in its vastness, retreat
To a hidden corner; without mercy guard
Its secret life as if a fortune were yours.

Lullaby for Ann-Lucian

My mother sliced the south for us.
She divided a poison from the flesh.
And every bite made the farmer laugh.

But your golden parents are oceanic
Touching lands my mother never knew.
A lighthouse keeps you off the rocks

Shine: though the fruit is foreign
Leave the rind. And don't swallow
The seeds, or you'll wake up a crow.

When an enemy of the harvest arrives
The country children use sling-shots.
They recognize his color and his greed.

Sunday

for Sam Allen

After awhile and by and by
I stood quiet . . .
But my soul got loud so I had
To shout.

One by one they called him
And the ushers came to fan them.

Take it easy Jesus, she's old and slow.
Don't bend her, breaking her down
Like she was a twig.

Near the cross, nearer, nearer

He sees your every move.
Pharaoh's army got the bad news.

Tremble, Jesus makes me tremble

The air was jungle thick.
I stood and said I'm a stranger
And Christ glowed
Within the stained-glass windows.

Take it easy Jesus . . .

It was hot and the sisters
Between forty and death
Fell into thought
With a thud.

Tremble, Jesus makes me tremble

One by one they called him
And the ushers came to fan them.

Near the cross, nearer, nearer

A little bit of Jesus is just enough.
She plays a mean tambourine,
A mean tambourine.

Blue Monday

Cotton eyes soaking up blood

All alone in Eskimo city
Cold and unsure, the music man

No earth angel, no sissy, brings
The night to its knees. Some-
Times he feels he's been below deck

All his life chained to a stranger
Moaning blue monday where's a calendar

Without weekends. Blue monday he moans
Where's a place where the darkness
Is not a dungeon. Slipping sliding his way

To be alive, he mumbles to his boss.
His soul trails behind him like a sled.

Too weak to work he's tired of playing.

He's gonna rock on the river of time
And stare at God until he goes blind.

Maybelle

Squeezed next to her sponge cakes
I hold my nuts too tight.
Her children dance before us
Rising like vapors
From the summer sidewalks.

There's not much room
On the steps and we're crowded
Together like peas
In a pod; childbirth made
Her soft, fat, and easy to get along with

As she nurses her fifth
Child, a boy who sucks like a plunger.
We're protected just by being
Here; if a bomb fell
There would be no survivors.

These night people will keep me
From myself; good barbecue
And beer, late mornings, moon sweat,
Lay ahead. All I remember is
The hop-scotch pattern of her braids.

Sister now five times a momma
Dreaming of hitting that magic number,
A combination. Her name
Isn't Maybelle but it might as well be.
She was/is so fine

Yes indeed I wanted her to be mine.
Her breasts are like crows
And her nipples aren't pink
But are more like sweet raisins
Dark against her son's darker mouth.

Killer Blues

Blackbird, blackbird, where's
Your nest now that Mister Rat ate

Your family and made a widower
Out of you? Hide higher than the sky

Next time. I'm housing one
Broken baby sucking can milk from pieces

Of bread; but it won't live long.
Two bitten wings, and wet bread isn't

His mother. Mister Rat feasted,
He found you out in the red barn eaves;

And now blackbird you pick up
Feathers, a new nest, a dumb blackbride.

Some men will say it was his
Last supper and conscience his cross.

Who gave him a soul, why are you
Flying in circles as if you were a hawk?

Outside the City

The fields are darker than dimples
Streaking in a curving line
To a hollow home.

On my side of the map mud softens
Like a forgotten face; acres
Of wheat bow like heads

Of slaves and away from here people
With my mind are politicians.
Breathing the pollen

Burns my eyes; the yard's drying
Crust cracks like a spine
Broken by burdens.

The darkies are laughing; the fence
Rots like the hull we sailed
In: we see it when

Memory serves us right. Birds sing bass
And the mountains look like
Scraped knuckles.

III

Beginning Again

I danced like a centipede going
A hundred different ways
To the tune of my father's whistle.
With his maddening mind
He sought his luck

In better things than love.
He was soon swaying with glee
At the sight of himself and lapsed
Into sitting moored to space.
My father mumbled
Himself into the scenery.

His life is my motto.
I live with the memory of a drunk's
Gait as he blows
His breath across the doorway.
I grow back again; I must

Be the dunce, the seventh son,
And smooth back my hair
Until I'm bald at the wounded breast.
Coughing up blood and supper
My sly father fades away.
I turn toward emptiness, chasing his scent.

Poem on My Birthday

Hawaii, 1969

Let the juices of watermelons sparkle
Be candles near the shore. Yesterday's
Rind is today's nostalgia. Listen —
Save the black seeds. and please laugh

At your face. Gingerly I return thinking
To my waking home: the evening is everyone.
The women come, and stay muzzled talking
Of me. I bless the women. They rise

And they cheer themselves with local color.
One woman eats a slice, asks me to design
A mouth for her that's broad, black, smiling.
One she can take off, admire as if it were

A painting. Let the juices of watermelons
Sparkle on shore. My lucky love will fathom
My retreating mind. The sea comes to my window
And watches. Women and children gladly follow.

If I Were Your Man

Your flannel gown could become silk!
Your red eyes light up the night like
An exit sign. Don't cry yourself to sleep
And lock your knees together to safe-
Guard your money-maker as if you were

A banker. Those volcanic sobs you hear
Rock the bed the way a man could if he
Were allowed inside. Honey bun! Honey bun!
Your mother's only girl, now you're sad
And bad to yourself, and twice as sweet.

Like wine these juices bubble with age
And the first one in the door won't get
Up any more. Your twins snore in the next
Room, and you remember pushing again with
Finesse; and you cuss your jet-black old

Man as the same pain the same sweat but no
Pleasure glues you to the sheets. Yes this is
Your life now each night as you lay the kids
Down, their wooly heads too prickly, their
Feet still kicking as they protest the hour.

But you can cradle me dear; I'm the only one.
I'm the one with the longest hands, the man
Who lies in your mind. Sweetness you got apples
Peaches oranges: let me pick your fruit, let
Me squeeze your lemons let me be your man.

Good Morning Blues

I'm fancied by your leech who
Owns my rooms.

With a hit like mine center
Hasn't a chance!

Who stole my blues, did I give
Them away?

I walk softly, buy a map,
But lady my blues

You're gone to another man.

Go read me in your bible,
Pronounce my name.

Who's lost! My body is home
And debt. I work,

Bring it back, and you're gone
Again. Hungry I hear

The bottom voices ask for rent.

Here's my knife: you be the shining
Thief who steals me.

Europe

is endowed with the first move,
Initiative enough to enhance to
A minimal edge; then element
Enters the game and many lovers
End in a draw. In almost every

Battle play positional with their
King. The traditional pawn breaks
Castles, achieves early equality
And wins but his heart is empty.

For the apex is the assault: drive
The enemy queen to a bad beginning
And later their romantic rook
Is shunted. Black commands the
Salient lines, the projected angles.

Resignation is justified only if
Followed by your mate. Europe hangs
On to the ghost. The blacks cross
Themselves and win. Can you see how?

The Poet's Shuffle

They applaud at the periods and sigh
During the commas.
My poems are full of carefully wrought pauses.
I read aloud until they yawn.

Should I growl or stomp my feet —
Maybe let my wrist go limp like a snake
On the edge of the podium?
But manlike I refuse to say another word.

They think I pout, that I'm sensitive,
Similar to a worm who grows again when hurting
Most. And they whisper walking out.
Man their polite smiles can cut!

I hear them say forgive the Negro
For he knows not what to do.
For a sentimental moment, the way Bo Jangles
Used to dance, I lift my big feet

And I do the poet's shuffle.
And then like Ben Jonson I recite:
My best poem is my son
And to each Shirley Temple I will give one.

But the old ladies in the front row
Will only give me the clap.
Like cannibals well fed they sleep and burp.
And I to my wife or mistress flee.

God Don't Like Ugly

Fantasy people are sad jigsaw
Puzzles, nightmares and daydreams.
Shattered lives spread across centuries
Like crumbs thrown to pigeons who

Stand in the cold passive in so much
Real shit, their own and everybody else's.
How many times have you put vaseline on
Your face, the winter making you grey

As a confederate uniform; and the wind
Drawn tears on your face leaves a thin grey
Line marching to your mouth. And you
Wonder where the black went cause it was

Time to carry the kerosene can back home.
If you spilled any you would smell for weeks
Because you didn't have a change of pants.
You can laugh now in the alley drinking

Some suds or complaining about the price
Of the grape. You can't follow in your father's
Footsteps because he never went anywhere
And you talk about tomorrow as if you cared.

People these times have killed your subtle
Imagination; no longer can you sing away riddles
As if they were wounds you could patch up.
Yes we're a fantasy people we're a sad people.

Hand Me Down Blues

for my brother George
1933–1971

Though I look like you
I never knew you very well.
You always confuse my slow shadow
And mock my fate.

I wear your defeats, limp or strut,
Even lie like you.
And I grow to fit your fears:
The carnivorous marriage,

And you swallowing a soft poison
Prescribed for healing
Only minor wounds.
I inherit new and old scars,

Dimples and warts; I am the residue
Of your black waste, its sin.
I am what remains
Beyond hunger or repair,

Your dead-ringer.
The worst lie is to say good-bye.
Where are you going that I won't follow?
My best is full of holes.

IV

For My Mother

Pale as the familiar cream and tea, you
Float past history and into a cup; before
My birth, a time so unreal I imagine
Helen stealing your thoughts while you
Decide to climb down for the favors
Of my father: he insisted that you charm
The sheriff and harness a mule for a free
Ride north. One brother was born already.

Drowning now as tired dreams like hands
Lift the fallen gay parade, you drink to a mad
Life father led leaving you always pregnant and poor.
Some sons went unborn. I was out on the final knot
Of promises, as your citadel collapsed in old age
And my lonely father became a fabled and alien man.

Father

Father father you're home safe
With one eye closed
Shut like a mousetrap.
Near death
You're nearer to my bone.

You lay in a hospital thin
As a worm and worried
Momma greyer;

Your ashy skin like wax
Drippings hung off
You and you lost yourself
In the night gambling
With nothing to show.

I can't imagine you tame
Like a stranger
Almost blind
Asking instead of taking.

I can't imagine you
Meek or silent.
Something caught inside
You hang on

And remain father father
And nearer to my bone.

M.A.P.

for Marcia

They can have your thighs,
Your ripe behind;
And even your Ibo eyes.
Or trade your breast on Wall Street.

But give me your mouth.
Save that for me
So I might hear you singing.

Even your tasty labia,
Delicate as the petals of a flower,
Can't speak as well

As the mouth
Below the plateau of your nose.
Send me your lips C.O.D.

And I will crown you Dancing Mouth
For your lips
Mambo across my face.

You may die,
But will me your bright mouth.
You may visit your Mother
At the basin of the Nile —

But surely you are kind enough
To leave my source
With me?

Or should I get a prescription
For a chastity belt
For your lips?

Or insure them under Lloyds of London?
Or form an organization
With the good acronym M.A.P.

her Mouth Always Pleases —
And claim we're charitable
And tax-exempt?

Noah's Dove

Child be out there: don't be surprised
Turn around and see who's watching who.
The raven raided, he left us; why wait?

I can't thumb my way across the river
When fish turn their mouths away; even
Lilies, the soft steps, break and float

Toward sea. They leave the meatless
Weeds sticking up like hair. I saw
A bird dive, he's been on board a body

Before. This summer the court ladies
Sit in folding chairs peeling skin.
Child be out there: don't be surprised.

Move

My limbs are dusty, come
Dust me boy; be
Good to baby.

She says it moving her lips
As she does her hips:
Not a word heard.

It's a dance, a tale told
In silence with an artful air
Of happy sin.

My limbs are dusty, come
Dust me boy; be
Good to baby.

Wipe it away.
A fire, a leaping light, it
Makes a mind sweat.

Her body is a magnet.
And you wish
You were harder than steel.

My limbs are dusty, come
Dust me boy; be
Good to baby.

The Middle Life

The brown shingles flap
Like Mister Sam's worn-out drawers.
The down man below me
Regrooves his voice to sing

A blues; the rain damns me in.
Mother moves without her
Shoes; children listen to themselves
During our Sunday quiet time.

The girl above dances
And her steps pry open the ceiling crack
That grins like a crocodile.
I'm caught in the middle

Of this sandwich, waiting.
Our Sunday house shines; there's no
Place to hide; the faster I pray
The slower I go. I'm breath-

Less; the air is like a noose.
It's my middle life, the uncool time
Between sin and salvation.
The rain damns me in.

Reading Walt Whitman

I found his wool face, I went away
A crook; there were lines I followed
When his song like a whistle led me.

Daily my wooden words fell, a parade
Of sticks, a broom bent over a thief's
Head. But then along came Langston

The proper shepherd who sat on history
Missing our music, dividing me; after
His death I rewrote, I robbed, and hid

In a foxhole until my lines were wood
On top, and soft underneath the bark.
Good Langston sat too long to lift me.

New Blues

for Jane

Day in day out like a wallflower,

Miss Moon, the lonely lightbody,
She's sleeping while I dig my hole.

No one to believe in, no one
To dance with, Missy wants to die.

I'm sorry but here I'm earning nothing
And wanting things God didn't invent.
Missy, I tell you you betta quick

Grow up. Decide your mind before
The doctor remembers we're not dead.

And before they raise the rent, enjoy
My love; under my covers what if I take

A flashlight and read me a dirty book?

Missy you listening? Don't worry.
You show only one side to me.

A dark man shall see dark days Missy.

Hope Against Hope

a poet's life

Nothing affects the genius of hope.
And the hum of hope keeps you awake at
Night; it shouts in your soul
And you want to kill it.

But hope comes back from its corner.
And you lie on the floor turning
Your ear away. Still you hear its hum
And you think suicide seeing

The open window: is it time for you
To die? Then heroes tease you and dangle
Hope in front of your bloodshot eyes.
It's a long way to Siberia and you try to

Hide in the wrinkles of your dirty hands.
This is the memoir of a master poet,
A hermit who was led away and pushed by
Hoodlums of hope who did him in.

No sleep, just skin, and no sweater; no
Love, only the paper-thin skin.
It's the genesis of poetry: words
Rising like goosebumps as you shudder.

Now you got rhythm and mumble words.
Each word picked up, kept or discarded,
Your lips moving like a guillotine.
You shake, you bite your breath, you scream.

You are doomed to walk down your shadow
Until you come to the end of your
Darkness. There you shall quote human
Feelings as you touch them in transit.

Some Pieces

When two elephants fight
It's only the grass that suffers

In the land of nod
Coke is king and scag god

I'm going I'm gone
Baby look what you've done
Left me and now day has come

The statues of some people never smile
Buddha does like a senile grandmother

Between us the bread was always stale

Should I lay my head on railroad tracks
Or should I lay my head on your wide lap

They can't plow the river
Snow lies on everything except
The road and it's black black

If I were a catfish swimming
In the deep blue sea
I'd start all you women
Jumping in after me

Somebody's in my bed
And they got my long johns on
I don't mind you taking my woman
But you better take my long johns off

And the white hand
Which bought me here
Which I learnt to hold
Now pushes me off the cliff

You can go home now

Your fingers are negroes
They do all the work for your fat arms